LET'S LEARN ABOUT...
THE OCEAN

BIG BOOK

K1

TRIXIA VALLE

Pearson Education Limited
KAO Two, KAO Park, Harlow, Essex, CM17 9NA, England
and Associated Companies around the world.

© Pearson Education Limited 2020

First published 2020

ISBN: 978-1-292-33412-7

Set in Mundo Sans
Printed in China (SWTC/01)

Acknowledgements
The publishers and author(s) would like to thank the following people and
institutions for their feedback and comments during the development of the
material: Marcos Mendonça, Leandra Dias, Viviane Kirmeliene, Gisele Aga,
Rhiannon Ball, Simara H. Dal'Alba, Mônica Bicalho and GB Editorial.
The publishers would also like to thank all the teachers who contributed to the
development of *Let's learn about...*: Adriano de Paula Souza, Aline Ramos Teixeira
Santo, Aline Vitor Rodrigues Pina Pereira, Ana Paula Gomez Montero, Anna
Flávia Feitosa Passos, Camila Jarola, Celiane Junker Silva, Edegar França Junior,
Fabiana Reis Yoshio, Fernanda de Souza Thomaz, Luana da Silva, Michael Iacovino
Luidvinavicius, Munique Dias de Melo, Priscila Rossatti Duval Ferreira Neves,
Sandra Ferito, and schools that took part in Construindo Juntos.

Author Acknowledgements
Trixia Valle

Image Credit(s):
Pearson Education Ltd: Francisco Domínguez 4, 5, 6, 20, 21, 22, Gerardo Sánchez
23, 24, 25, 26, Ismael Vázquez 17, 18, 19, Jesús Urueta 11, 12, 13, Leticia Morales
14, 15, 16, Marcela Gómez 7, 8, 9, 10, Víctor Sandoval 27, 28, 29, 30; **Shutterstock.
com:** Ekkasit Rakrotchit 20, 22, Frantisek Czanner 20, 21, 22, HelloRF Zcool 20, 22

Illustration Acknowledgements
Illustrated by Filipe Laurentino and MRS Editorial

Cover illustration © Filipe Laurentino

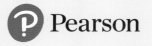

CONTENTS

U1   AN IMPORTANT FIRST DAY   4

U2   WE LOVE GYM!   7

U3   A VISITOR FROM MARS   11

U4   LOLA'S TOYS   14

U5   THE ELVES' HOUSE   17

U6   IKU THE FISH   20

U7   CAREFUL WITH THE SPAGHETTI!   23

U8   WHAT DO YOU LIKE ABOUT SCHOOL?   27

READING STRATEGIES   31

AN IMPORTANT FIRST DAY

KARLA LOVES TO BE WITH MOM. THEY PLAY AND SING ALONG.

MOM SAYS, "MAKE NEW FRIENDS AT SCHOOL."

"SAY *THANK YOU, PLEASE,* AND FOLLOW THE RULES."

"THIS IS KARLA," MISS TAYLOR SAYS.
THE STUDENTS LOOK AT HER.

KARLA IS SHY.
SHE WANTS TO HIDE!

"SIT DOWN, KARLA," SAY HER FRIENDS. THEY SHARE THEIR COLORED PENS.

TIME TO GO! BYE-BYE!

MARTIN LOVES SPORTS.

HE LIKES SPORTS AND BALLS.

HE HAS LONG ARMS AND BIG HANDS.

HE CAN CATCH BALLS WITH HIS LONG ARMS.

HE CAN CATCH BALLS WITH HIS BIG HANDS.

JANE LOVES RUNNING.

SHE LIKES RUNNING ON THE GRASS.

SHE HAS LONG LEGS.

SHE IS VERY FAST WITH HER LONG LEGS.

SHE IS A GOOD RUNNER.

TINA LOVES GYMNASTICS.

SHE LIKES WALKING ON THE BAR.

SHE CAN TOUCH HER FEET WITH HER HANDS.

SHE IS VERY FLEXIBLE.

SHE HAS FUN.

ALL THE CHILDREN LOVE GYM.
THEY CAN GO OUTSIDE.
THEY CAN PLAY ON THE GRASS.
THEY LOVE THE SHINING SUN.
OH, EVERY DAY IS A BEAUTIFUL DAY!

A VISITOR FROM MARS

MY FAMILY AND I ARE TOGETHER.

"LOOK," SAYS DAD. "A SPACESHIP!"

A LITTLE GREEN MARTIAN COMES OUT OF IT.

"HELLO! WHO ARE YOU?"

"WE ARE A FAMILY," I SAY.

"THIS IS DAD. THIS IS MOM.

THIS IS MY BIG BROTHER.

AND THIS IS SHOO, OUR DOG."

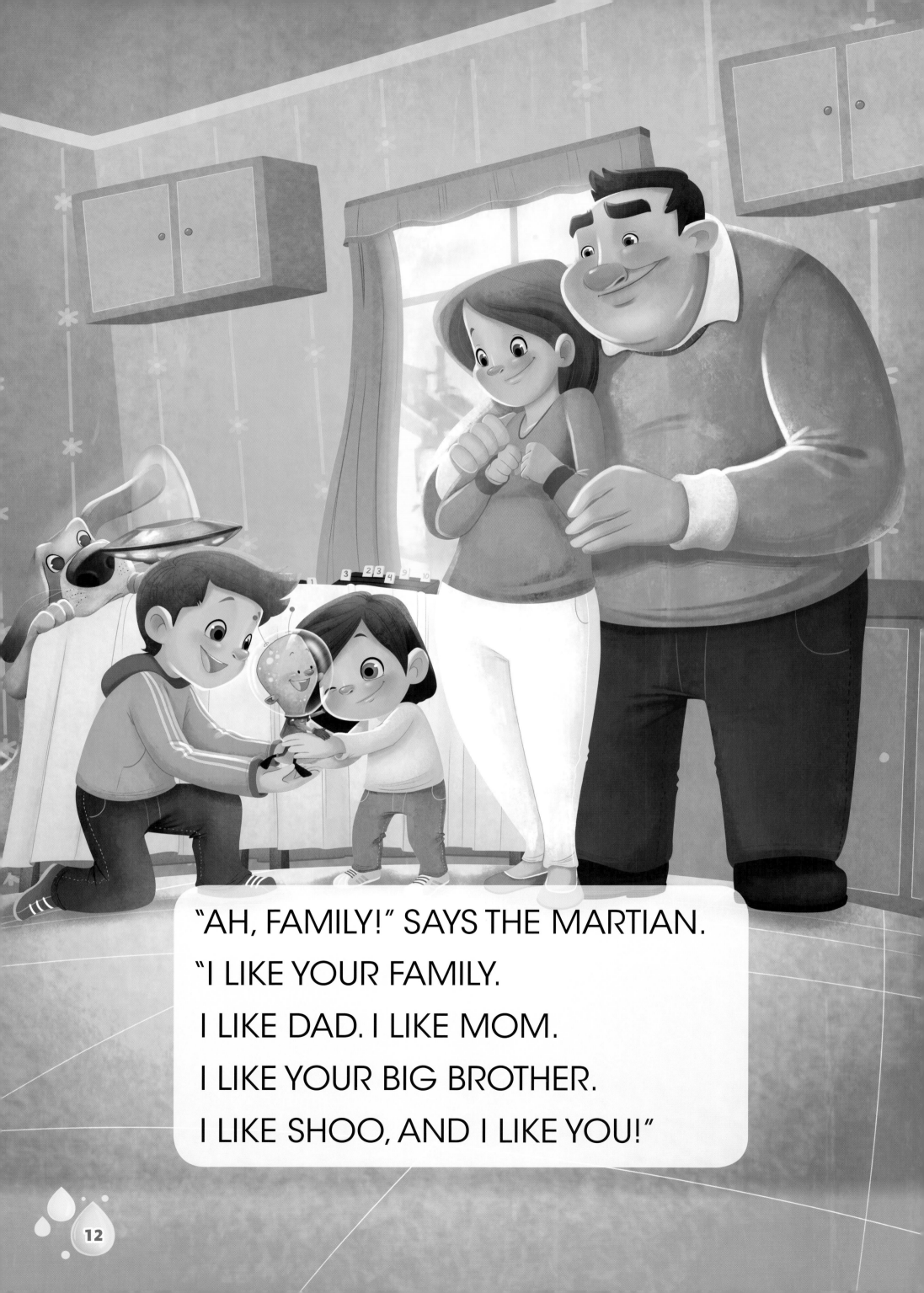

"AH, FAMILY!" SAYS THE MARTIAN.

"I LIKE YOUR FAMILY.

I LIKE DAD. I LIKE MOM.

I LIKE YOUR BIG BROTHER.

I LIKE SHOO, AND I LIKE YOU!"

"CAN I BE A PART OF YOUR FAMILY?"
ASKS THE MARTIAN.

WE ALL LAUGH. WE ARE HAPPY.

MOM AND DAD HUG THE MARTIAN HELLO.

BROTHER AND SHOO SAY HELLO, TOO.

THE MARTIAN IS PART OF OUR FAMILY NOW.

LOLA'S TOYS

LOLA LOVES HER TOYS.
SHE HAS LOTS OF TOYS.
THE TOYS ARE PRETTY AND CLEAN.
SOME OF HER TOYS ARE NEW.

HER FRIENDS COME TO PLAY,
BUT SHE PUTS THE TOYS AWAY.

SHE LIKES HER TOYS
PRETTY AND CLEAN.

HER FRIENDS GO AWAY!

LOLA IS SAD.

DAD SAYS, "LOLA DEAR, SHARE YOUR TOYS WITH YOUR FRIENDS.

PLAYING TOGETHER IS MORE FUN."

THE NEXT DAY LOLA'S FRIENDS COME TO PLAY.

SHE DOESN'T PUT HER TOYS AWAY.

THEY ALL PLAY TOGETHER.

HER TOYS ARE NOT CLEAN, BUT LOLA IS VERY HAPPY!

THE ELVES' HOUSE

THIS IS SAM AND DEB'S HOUSE.

THERE IS A GARDEN IN FRONT OF THE HOUSE.

AND IN THE GARDEN, THERE IS A LITTLE GARDEN.

A SECRET GARDEN…

IN THE SECRET GARDEN,
THERE IS A LITTLE HOUSE.

A LITTLE HOUSE WITH A GREEN DOOR.

THIS LITTLE HOUSE IS THE ELVES' HOUSE.

WHEN SAM AND DEB PLAY TOGETHER,
THEY ALWAYS LOOK THROUGH THE WINDOWS.

AND WHAT DO THEY SEE?

THEY SEE ELVES CLEANING THE HOUSE:

ONE SWEEPS THE FLOOR.

ANOTHER CLEANS THE WINDOWS.

TWO ELVES SET THE TABLE.
ONE SETS THE PLATES ON THE TABLE.
THE OTHER PLACES THE SPOONS.

EVERYBODY IS HAPPY.
THEY SIT AND EAT TOGETHER.
SAM SAYS, "EVERYBODY HELPS AT HOME."
DEB SAYS, "BECAUSE IT IS EVERYBODY'S HOME."

IKU THE FISH

THE BIG FISH TANK HAS WONDERFUL THINGS.

THE WATER IS TRANSPARENT AND BLUE.

THERE IS A DIVER.

THERE ARE PLANTS AND FLOWERS.

THERE ARE MANY COLORFUL FISH.

ERIC'S FAVORITE FISH IS IKU.
IKU IS A BIG PURPLE FISH.
IKU IS THE KING FISH.
ALL THE LITTLE FISH FOLLOW IKU.

ERIC LIKES IKU.

HE LIKES THE LITTLE FISH.

HE FEEDS THE FISH.

HE TAKES CARE OF THEM.

MOM AND GRANDMA ARE VERY PLEASED.

MOM SAYS, "ERIC TAKES CARE OF HIS PETS. HE IS RESPONSIBLE."

GRANDMA SAYS, "VERY GOOD, ERIC!"

ERIC IS VERY HAPPY.

CAREFUL WITH THE SPAGHETTI!

THIS IS AN ITALIAN RESTAURANT.

MOM, DAD, AND TESS ARE AT THE TABLE.

THEY WANT SPAGHETTI.

THEY ARE HUNGRY.

"WHAT IS THAT?" ASKS TESS.

MOM SAYS, "IT'S A BIB. IT'S TO KEEP YOUR CLOTHES CLEAN."

"WHY?" ASKS TESS.

"MY SHIRT IS NEW AND IT'S CLEAN," SAYS DAD. "THE BIB KEEPS MY SHIRT CLEAN."

"WHY?" ASKS TESS.

"BECAUSE SPAGHETTI IS DIFFICULT TO EAT!" LAUGH MOM AND DAD.

TESS SAYS, "MY DRESS IS NEW AND IT'S CLEAN.

I WANT MY DRESS CLEAN. SPAGHETTI IS DIFFICULT TO EAT. I WANT A BIB!"

MOM AND DAD LAUGH.

NOW MOM, DAD, AND TESS ARE EATING SPAGHETTI.

"BE CAREFUL WITH THE SPAGHETTI," SAY MOM AND DAD.

"SPAGHETTI IS DIFFICULT TO EAT, BUT MY DRESS IS CLEAN!" SAYS TESS.

WHAT DO YOU LIKE ABOUT SCHOOL?

LAURA GOES TO SCHOOL.

IT IS HER FIRST DAY AT SCHOOL.

THE SCHOOL IS VERY BIG.

THERE ARE MANY CLASSROOMS.

THERE ARE MANY TEACHERS.

THE SCHOOL YARD IS VERY BIG.

LAURA WANTS TO GO HOME.
SHE WANTS TO BE WITH MOM.
"LOOK!" SAYS MOM. "A SLIDE."

LAURA GOES TO PLAY.
MOM AND MISS SMITH SMILE.

LAURA GOES BACK.

SHE SAYS, "MOM, I WANT TO STAY. I WANT TO PLAY WITH THE CHILDREN."

MOM KISSES LAURA GOODBYE.

"LET'S GO AND PLAY," SAYS MISS SMITH.

THERE ARE MANY CHILDREN IN THE SANDBOX.

THEY PLAY TOGETHER.

LAURA PLAYS WITH THE CHILDREN.

"I LIKE TO PLAY WITH FRIENDS!" SAYS LAURA.

"I LIKE SCHOOL."

Reading Strategies

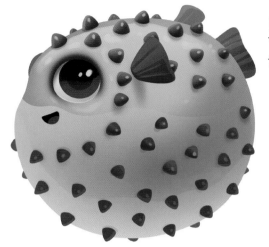

Bring as many books as you want to the classroom. Prepare a corner for reading. You can have students bring their favorite pillow and allow them to lie down while they "read" or explore a book.

- Before showing the corresponding text to students, present a situation similar to that in the book so students begin thinking about it and relate it to their own experiences and knowledge.

- Have students work in pairs or small groups to share their ideas with the whole group. They can also imagine a scene and draw it.

- Show the title, subtitle (if there is one), and illustrations on the title page, and ask students to predict what the story is about. Allow them to speculate and accept all ideas.

- You can show students the text and illustrations and ask if they know anything about the topic.

- Ask one or two questions related to the story, so students listen for the answers or can infer them.

- Once students have become familiarized with the story, ask them to summarize it briefly.

- Put the scenes on construction paper or cardboard, and cut out the pictures of each scene so students can put the story in order. Have students work in pairs for this activity.

Unit 1

An important first day

Activities with students

1. Ask students how they feel when they go to school.
2. Have students notice that they can feel different things.
3. Reflect on the importance of being respectful when somebody has a different opinion.

Unit 2

We love gym!

Activities with students

1. Ask students how we are all similar.
2. Ask them how we are all different.
3. Have students notice that some children are good at some activities and others are good at other activities.
4. Reflect on the importance of being respectful about differences.

Unit 3

A visitor from Mars

Activities with students

1. Have students reflect on their families. Encourage them to talk about the members of their family.
2. In groups of three or four, have them reflect on the differences in their families: how many brothers, sisters, grandparents, who they live with, etc.
3. Reflect with students that although families are different, they are loving people and we have to accept all differences.

Unit 4

Lola's toys

Activities with students

1. Ask students what toys they have.
2. Have them work in groups of four and say how they feel when they break or lose a toy.
3. Encourage them to say how they take care of their toys.
4. Elicit how important it is to share.

Unit 5

The elves' house

Activities with students

1. Ask students who helps in their house.
2. Have them work in groups of three. Ask them how they help in the house.
3. Encourage them to think if it is better to work together or individually. Ask why.
4. Ask students to think about how they feel after they have helped at home.

Unit 6

Iku the fish

Activities with students

1. Ask students to talk about their pets and pets they would like to have. Have them say if their pets feel happy or not, and how they know how their pet feels.
2. In groups of three, have students say how they can take care of pets.
3. Ask them to think about how we can respect our pets and our friends' pets.

Unit 7

Careful with the spaghetti!

Activities with students

1. In groups of three or four, ask students what their favorite food is.
2. Encourage them to say what food they don't like.
3. Ask students what they do when they don't like something to eat.
4. Tell them to notice the similarities and differences in their likes and dislikes. Reflect with students that they have to be respectful about others' opinions.

Unit 8

What do you like about school?

Activities with students

1. In groups of three or four, have students say what their favorite activity at school is.
2. Ask them if they know all the people who work at school.
3. Reflect with students that people at school help them feel safe and happy.
4. Talk about the importance of being grateful to these people.